D1274607

Contents

N2
12389

Introduction to Quilts

The needlework art of quilting is documented back some 3,000 years in a carved ivory figure of an Egyptian king whose regal garments definitely reveal a quilted pattern. This figure is in the British Museum. As textiles are a fragile medium, source material to substantiate the origin with any certainty is extremely limited.

A carpet found on the floor of a tomb during the Koslov expedition in 1924-25 has been dated no later than the 2nd century A.D. and is the earliest example of quilting to survive to date. The application and intricacy of the spiral and scroll patterns are not unlike those being currently employed. The piece is in the holdings of the Academy of Sciences in Leningrad.

Quilting was recorded in the Far East for more than 2,000 years before trade involvement brought the art to Europe. It is from this area that diverse innovations have been recorded with some accuracy.

It was during the harsh winters of the 14th century that European women seriously considered quilting as a necessity against the cold. The tripart technique was influenced by quilted armor introduced by the Crusaders when they returned from the Asiatic marches. Crude at best, these pieces were void of artistic traits. Unrefined anchor stitches held the warm yet cumbersome pieces together. They much resembled the pallet on which one slept rather than later masterful renditions in the same technique.

Traditionally the finest materials and workmanship have been reserved for the church and royalty. Following the expulsion of the Moors from southern Spain, when the country became an intensely unified Catholic country, fine quilting for the adornment of ecclesiastical vestments reached a high degree of excellence. Somewhat later the inventory of Charles V included "16 quilted silken nightshirts."

In the kingdom of the Two Sicilies the oppressive climate resulted in decorative rather than utilitarian quilting. Three quilts from this section of Italy are known to exist today. Of these, two were obviously made as a pair although they have been separated. One of the pair, and the only complete example, is in the Victoria and Albert Museum in London. The other one is in the collection of the Bargello in Florence. The third quilt is also in Florence in a private collection. The legendary life of Tristam is depicted similarly in all three.

These pieces, with their heavily embossed designs, are particularly significant in that they illustrate the process of "trapunto" credited to the Italians. In this technique once the pattern has been established, the outline is stitched where the padding is desired. From the backside, threads are separated to allow tiny wads of cotton to be forced into the area until the desired puff is achieved. All three of the Sicilian pieces are worked in brown and natural thread backstitched through the two layers of heavy linen. A like technique developed in England is referred to as "white on white." The New England colonists perpetuated this white thread and white material method inherited from the motherland.

The blustery winters of the British Isles created a wide demand for quilting. Various types of wearing apparel, reinforced and decorated with quilting, were created in answer to this demand. Of these, the nightcap was most popular. Many examples of quilted garments have been documented, but it is not the purpose of this publication to do more than bring the existence of these records to the reader's attention.

The quilting represented in this publication deals exclusively with 19th and 20th century examples as exemplified in the collection of the Denver Art Museum. As with all quilting, the purpose is twofold: warmth and decoration. Construction is tripart with the top being the design (pieced or appliqued), the backing of the maker's choice and then the filling or stuffing. Unfortunately space does not allow for the illustration of all of the examples in the collection, but each category is well represented.

Imelda G. DeGraw
Curator of Textiles and Costumes

Pieced Quilts

The pieced quilts which originated in America are perhaps the most picturesque, illustrating the imagination of the early settlers. It was the Pilgrim women of New England who developed limitless patterns which are still being copied and improvised upon today. Quilt making traveled from the Northeast to Kentucky and Tennessee, then into the mountains of North and South Carolina and Virginia.

Designs were, by the very nature of the mode of life, variations of stars that lighted the skies, flowers common to the locality, birds, trees and the changing seasons.

Names of the patterns originated from regions and were strongly influenced by political events as well as significant social affairs. In some cases, a single pattern is known by several names as it traveled from place to place.

Although the pieced quilt is considered less difficult to make than the applique, it is tedious and exacting in that each piece must be perfectly cut and sewn. This "laid-out" process was performed by adults and when the patterns were deemed simple enough they were turned over to young ladies as a means of learning stitchery.

Dating and signing of quilts was not common practice. Thus dating must be based on the use of different materials in each period and the variations in the size of quilts. These distinctions will be referred to as they apply to the different quilts in this section of the catalogue.

1 and 1a
The maker of this quilt added to its complexity by selecting a multitude of different cotton prints to form each star. Little attention was given to the assemblage from the standpoint of color coordination. However, as is apparent in the color illustration on the opposing page, the deep red ground dotted with black serves as a unifying agent. Minute quilt stitches in diamond pattern are used throughout.
64 x 80 in.

A-1897
Gift of Mrs. Robert S. Ohlson

2 and 3

The star is among the most popular and also most difficult patterns in pieced quilts. Red and green calico on white is set five down and four across. The line and diagonal quilting which can be seen more clearly in the detail indicates a date c. 1830. This is a version of *Lemoyne Star,* also known as *Lemon Star.*
74 x 94 in.   A-609
                                      Gift of Mrs. Marion Byles Grove

4, opposing page

One hundred stars form the geometric layout of this quilt. Quaint calico in shades of turquoise, yellow and white is cut into squares for the star centers and eight triangles form the points. The extraordinary quilting adds yet another dimension of beauty.
75 in. square   A-895
                                From the Estate of Mrs. Ruth Mills Knapp

5 and 6

A variety of gingham, calico and percale in shades of gray are worked into another version of an eight-point star, known as the *Hanging Diamond*. Vibrant pink calico squares are alternated with the star squares. This material is dated by the donor as 1880. She referred to the color as "Norwegian pink." However, those currently researching textiles as a means of dating quilts find it documented as "seaweed" and it appears in many colors. Six stars form the width; seven the length; foursided border.

72 x 76 in.   A-373

Gift of Mrs. Charlotte Jane Whitehill

7 and 8

This cradle-size patchwork is made up of pieced squares with a star in each unit. Another example of the *Lemoyne Star,* this particular star pattern takes its name from the LeMoyne brothers — Pierre, who captured the three James Bay posts in Canada from the English in 1686, and Jean Baptiste, who founded New Orleans in 1718. The star quilt pattern which bore the family name was soon appropriated by other states, and the Yankee housewives, stumbling over the unfamiliar French pronunciation, called it the *Lemon Star.* The blocks, here set point-to-point against a background of darker tone, result in a zigzag line, as much a part of the pattern as the star itself. The calico ground is rose colored, and the stars are in multi-colored prints and stripes.

36 x 38 in.

A-220

Gift of Mrs. Helen Newbury

9, at left
Over 1200 diamond shapes in shades of green, yellow, blue, lavender and pink are interspersed with white to form this variation of the star pattern. Alternate squares are quilted in overlapping circle and plume patterns. The seven-inch border repeats the diamond pattern.
88 in. square   A-2094
                          Gift of Mrs. Thelma Johns

10, opposing page
Double Wedding Ring was a popular design in the early 1900's. It is a difficult design to draft because of the time comsuming process of matching rectangular pieces into circular forms. This example, reportedly from the northwest region of the United States, is unusual in background color. There is another quilt of the same pattern in the collection.
76 x 94 in.   A-2060
                       Gift of Irene Littledale Britton

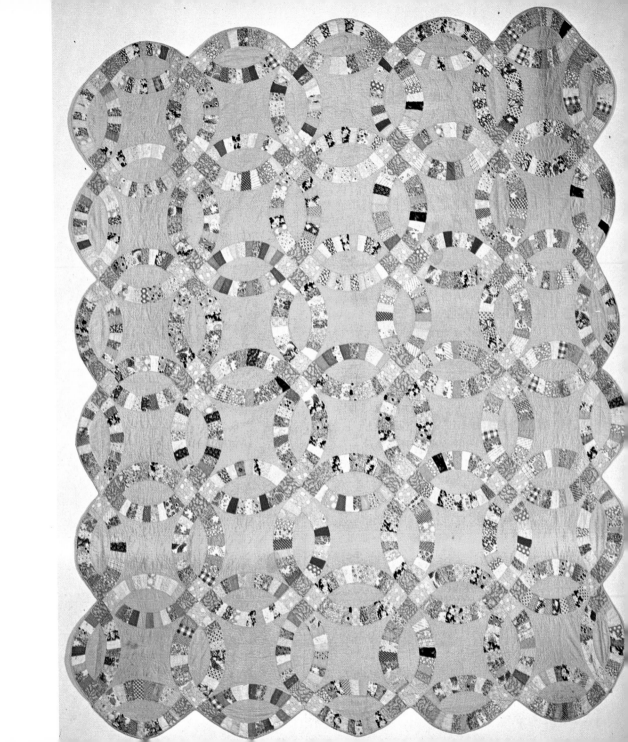

11 and 12

The squares in this quilt are one inch in size. Cut diagonally, they are interspersed with another calico resembling chicken wire. The result is rather subtle. The material is an excellent index of everyday dresses of the Civil War period because almost no complete costumes of daytime wear have survived. The quilt is composed of 17,424 pieces, and when viewed at long range, as in the more complete illustration on the opposing page, the rather primitive composition is transformed into an electrifying example of Op Art. A lavender calico backing and border add a nostalgic quality to the quilt, which dates from 1883.

76 in. square

A-560

Gift of Mrs. S. Effie Parkhill

13 and 14

Steeple Chase was made in 1865 by Mrs. Elizabeth Ann Cline. A composite of 20 different dark blue and white materials, the quilt is at first glance deceptively simple. However, in the detail illustrated above, there is evidence of a high degree of intricacy in the skillful piecing.

69 x 81 in.   A-690

   Gift of the artisan's daughter, Mrs. Charlotte Jane Whitehill

15 and 16

One of the truly old patterns sought by the collector is *Drunkard's Path,* also known under the designation of *Robbing Peter to Pay Paul*. It was a most popular pattern in the period 1825-50. The most usual color is "turkey red" worked in a chain effect on white. Quilting is of the simplest with no thought to a specific design.

86 in. square   A-735

Gift of Mrs. Frederic H. Douglas

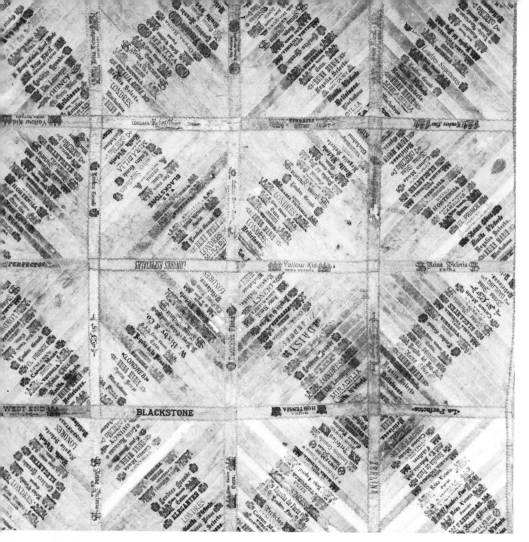

17, above
Silk cigar bands in various shades of gold are worked in four blocks either way, resulting in a unique and novel quilt throw.
48 in. square

A-1445
Gift of Mrs. Andrew Anderson

18, opposing page
A mosaic quilt of one-inch squares combines prints and solid cottons, creating a scenic rendition of the Matterhorn. This quilt was so described by the artist, Myrtle M. Fortner. Signed and dated, July, 1934, this quilt has been loaned to several major exhibitions, including the American Pavilion at Osaka, Japan.
168 x 204 in.

A-1437
Gift of Mr. Melvin C. Dorsett

19 and 20

English fabrics are preserved in this quilt inventoried over 150 years ago in the Biddle Reeves family records. An assemblage of wood-block prints and copperplate designs is quilted in diamond patterns which attach it to the handwoven linen backing. Such lightweight covering was for summer use. As seen in the overall illustration on the opposing page, the scenes of farm life which compose the border of the quilt are close in style to those of the printer John Collins of Woolmers, Hertfordshire, whose work is dated c. 1765. Shell and garland prints surround the center piece — a statue of Shakespeare.

75 x 95 in.

E-1021
Gift of Mr. Philip S. Van Cise

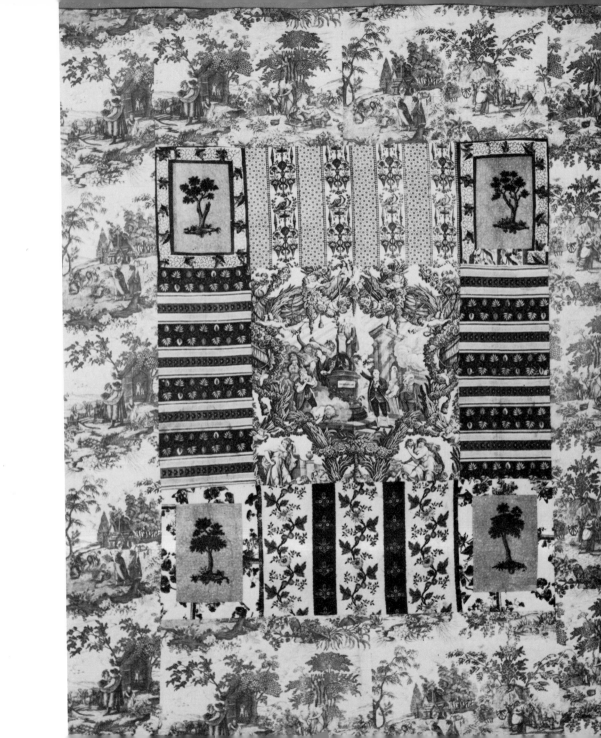

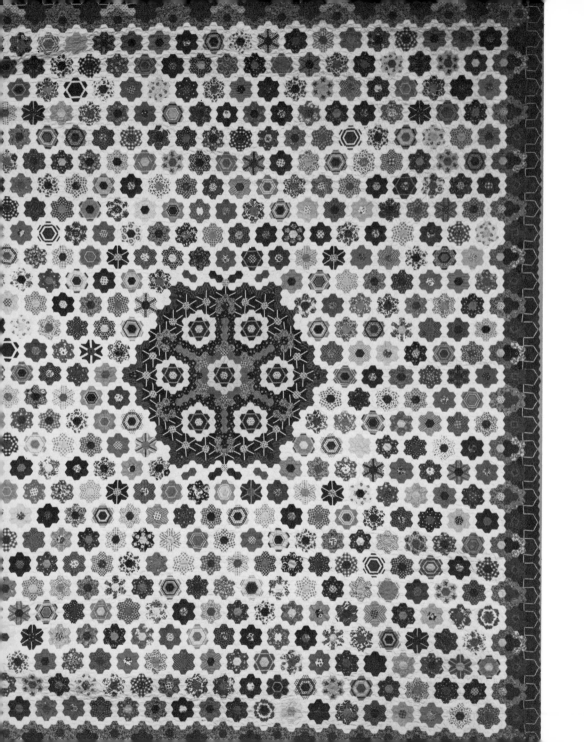

21, opposing page

Hexagon or *Honeycomb* is one of the more tedious patterns to achieve. When properly done, paper or pasteboard is cut to back each piece leaving just enough material to turn the edges under. These separate hexagons are then sewn into groups of seven, forming flower-like units. As the project progresses, a veritable flower garden results. Dr. Summerill's wife, Frances, copied the quilt from one in the collection of the Metropolitan Museum in New York City, and it was judged the best of pieced-work quilts at the New York State Fair in 1951.

The quilt is signed and dated 1940-50.
84 x 104 in.   A-1550
Gift of Dr. Frederick Summerill, Teaneck, New Jersey, in memory of his wife, Frances Hepp Summerill

22

This outstanding example of a Revolutionary period quilt, as the detail reveals, is composed of meticulously padded blocks of pattern, a technique known as trapunto. The textural effect comes from the masterful hand of an adroit seamstress. The pattern resulting from the regularly spaced squares of brown and white prints and early calicoes is known as *Double Nine Patch* or *Irish Chain.* Three sides of the quilt are finished with hand-knotted fringe. The initials "R.D." are worked into one of the padded squares. Although there is no date, 1775-1800 is a reasonable period of origin.
82 x 98 in.   A-607
Gift of Mrs. Marion Byles Grove

23, at left
Brocades and taffetas of the mid-1800's are worked into this quilt in the *Lincoln Log* pattern, made in 1880 by Lucy G. Tucker. This well-known design originating in Colonial days was recommended for the beginner. As in this example, tufting was often used to attach the three layers together.

68 x 72 in.   A-1776

Gift of Mrs. Minnie T. Moore

24, opposing page
Variations of the *Log Cabin* pattern are inexhaustible. These were popular after the Civil War, as they were a very economical way of utilizing the smallest fragments of material. *Courthouse Steps* was the name given to this particular arrangement of folded strips. Although worked in squares, the fret styling allows the viewer to see many different compositions.

66 x 54 in.   A-2126

Gift of Mrs. Regina L. Collins

25, at right
One of the simplest renditions of the *Log Cabin* quilt pattern is achieved by making individual squares from material fragments and sewing them together in opposite directions. In this piece, 80 five-inch squares are bordered with black satin. The border of the quilt is made of many shades of silk velvet fashioned in pointed scallops.
56 x 68 in.   A-2142
                    Gift of Mrs. Lennig Sweet

26, opposing page
In this quilt silk strips are worked out from velvet centers composed of four triangles forming a square. Centers differ in color as do the silk threads used in tufting. It was not uncommon to tuft such quilts rather than quilt them. Though a timesaving method, it added to rather than detracted from the pattern.
64 x 52 in.   A-2143
                    Gift of Mrs. Lennig Sweet

Crazy Quilts

This form of quilt making is strictly American. Filled with Victorian sentimentality, the hit-and-miss compositions of these masterpieces of 19th century stitchery are replete with memorabilia. The use of small scraps of material makes one aware of the tremendous value placed on each useable filament of silk, satin or velvet.

The usual construction was accomplished by piecing many odd shapes into squares which were then sewn together. Fantastic embroidery skills were applied in various decorative additions. The fan was one of the more popular but others included birds, umbrellas, names and dates reflecting tender attachments. Hand-painted motifs added a whimsical note with commemorative ribbons contributing other significant mementos.

Terminology is misleading as applied to these quilts, as few were actually quilted. Rather, they were tufted or tacked in a systematic design.

The craze for these zigzag type quilts was unique in the fact that, unlike the pieced quilts, sizes varied. Usually they were parlor throws, meant to be admired for the elaborate materials and rich embellishment.

The renewed interest in the crazy work quilt, which is in evidence today, results in most unconventional shapes and proportions when adapted to the contemporary environment. Of course, the 20th century quilt maker has a vast source of materials available for the designer's creative objective.

27 and 28

Well-planned composition takes this crazy quilt out of ordinary context. Multicolored satins and brocades were drafted into circles which were embellished with exquisite embroidery stitches in rich shades of silk floss. Interspersed velvet triangles add further beauty to this handsome fabric structure.

65 x 66 in.

A-2012

Gift of Mrs. William Woodward
Boulder, Colorado

29 and 30 and 31

Mrs. William N. Byers (Elizabeth Minerva Sumner), wife of the founder of *The Rocky Mountain News,* made this crazy quilt throw in the early 1890's prior to the birth of her son Alfred, whose name she later embroidered in metallic thread on one of the satin pieces. According to the donor, the son died at an early age. The family initial "B" dominates another silk piece. The fabrics are in superb condition probably as a result of the quilt being put into storage after the son's death. The number of masterful embroidery stitches is extensive.

32 x 66 in.

A-1405
Gift of Inna T. Aulls

32 and 33

Perhaps the most ornate of all the crazy quilts in the collection is this masterpiece in pristine condition. Luxurious fabrics in a rainbow of colors and prints make up the ground with each piece outlined in feather stitch. Many of the pieces are ornamented in solid satin stitch with a profusion of designs.

56 x 60 in.

A-2080
Mrs. Ralph Crandell

34 and 35
Members of Plymouth Daughters of the Congregational Church in Arkansas City, Kansas, executed this quilt in 1920. It was a common practice to give a quilt as a farewell gift to the wife of a departing pastor with each participant signing her name. In this instance the quilt is signed with the 17th century feminine names assumed by members of the group in honor of the Calvinist virtues. Non-members of the group signed their real names. Mrs. George T. Nichols was the recipient of the quilt when her husband left Kansas to become pastor of Berkeley Community Congregational Church in Denver. The quilt was donated to the Denver Art Museum by Mrs. Nichols' elder son. 86 x 140 in.   A-1899
Gift of Mr. and Mrs. Dean G. Nichols

36 and 37

Materials of more common use appear again in this simple crazy quilt. Darker colors and heavier textures suggest that the wools and cottons were from daytime clothing which adds another dimension of interest since very few everyday costumes have survived. The consistency of the feather stitching indicates the work of a single artisan. Made in Rexford, Kansas, in 1910. 76 x 69 in.

A-1925

Gift of Mr. and Mrs. Robert L. Johnson
in memory of his mother, Frieda H. Johnson

38 and 39

The use of many fine fabrics and the application of numerous techniques add greatly to the interest of this quilt. It was made in 1892 by Augusta Ernestine Houck, mother of the donor. Pieces from the gowns of wives of Colorado Governors Adams, Oram and Cooper are among those included. The black taffeta comes from the wedding gown of the donor's grandmother who was married in 1868. The detail below shows the scope of material selected as well as the embroidered teapot, cup and saucer in one area and a hand painted pear in another.

60 x 68 in.

A-1280

Gift of Mrs. Norris Miles

Appliqué Quilts

As the name implies, appliqué is the method of applying one material onto another by means of a stitch of the same name. This type of quilt-making prevailed shortly after the introduction of patchwork in America, reaching its zenith in the mid-1800's. The majority of appliqués in the Denver Art Museum collection came as a gift from Mrs. Charlotte Jane Whitehill, whose generous gift of 35 quilts in 1955 actually established this area of acquisition within the Textile Department. Additions during the subsequent years have been multitudinous.

Elaborate designs flourish in this technique as does the masterful selection of fabrics. The end result has often been likened to that of an artist approaching an easel. Rightfully so, when one considers the skill of drafting the pattern, the necessary care for the edges of each piece which must be meticulously turned under and applied to the base cloth. Points are especially hazardous! Precise details are manipulated, a process comparable to the selection of colors when creating a painting.

Although to date there are no examples in our collection, the Hawaiian appliqués warrant mention. In today's revival of quilting, these introduce several departures from the conventional approach to the art. Freehand designs are ordinarily a single, bold presentation executed in vibrant colors. A single artisan develops the entire piece which results in a consistency of workmanship. Also, quilting patterns are marked from the backside rather than the top as is familiar on the mainland. An industrious quilter can produce a full quilt in one month — surprisingly short time for the work involved.

Today's quilters are employing appliqué to produce many useful and decorative objects, such as placemats, potholders, tote bags, tennis racket covers and pillows. Participants are of all ages, as everyone is getting involved! During this past season the Textile Department presented an exhibition, *Fabrics and Techniques,* in which a program of demonstrations was an integral part of the display. Quilting and embroidery were among the techniques demonstrated, and the public response was entirely enthusiastic.

40 and 41

The origin of this quilt has been carefully documented and published by the donor, who was not only an excellent quilter but also a pioneer in collecting and printing information on the art. This particular example of a quilt in the *Prince's Feather* pattern was made in 1829 by Mary Black and is said to have been carried in a bride's chest from Kentucky to California during the gold rush of 1853. The stains which appear on the white ground resulted when the chest was thrown from an oxcart while crossing a stream en route. The red, green and yellow color combination appears frequently in quilts of this period. This was purchased by the donor in Paris, Kentucky, and patterned for reproduction as noted in *Mrs. Danner's Third Quilt Book,* 1954.

87 in. square

A-1915

Gift of Mrs. Scioto I. Danner, Newton, Kansas

42 and 43

Flowers were a great inspiration to the early quilter who created her own patterns from everyday surroundings. *Flower Baskets,* c. 1850, might leave the dedicated horticulturist at a loss to identify each blossom but the charm transmitted by the multiple blooms more than compensates. Blanket stitch outlines most of the flowers, while slanting quilt lines give a textural quality to the baskets. Feather pattern quilting fills in most of the open white spaces.

75 x 77 in.   A-155
Gift of Mrs. S. Effie Parkhill

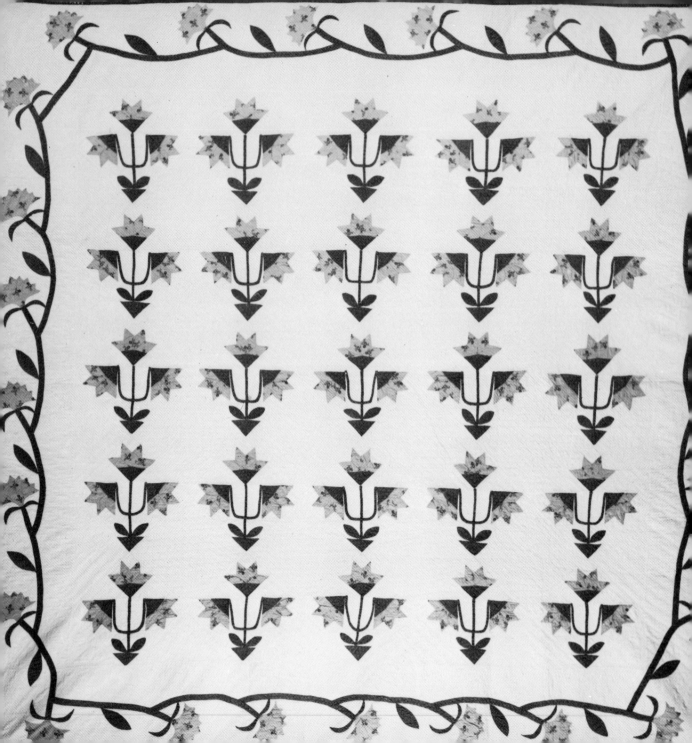

44 and 45

Virginia Lily is the name most often used to identify this quilt pattern, a name derived from a flower particularly well-liked in this period. Piecing is used in the blossom sections and appliqué for leaves and stems. The early calicoes employed indicate a date of about 1830. The quilting is done in squares with the exception of the heart patterns in each of the four corners. This corner motif was associated with bride quilts.
81 x 80 in.

A-222
Museum Purchase

46 and 47

Documentation accompanying this quilt credits the original pattern to the Martindale family and dates it c. 1840. The family was reportedly very reluctant to share this treasure which had been made in Burlington, Vermont. The combination of printed percales is an artistic achievement in itself. One then marvels at the tedious padding in the quilting patterns which are of a most elaborate detail. This quilt again reveals the remarkable ingenuity and ability of the early quilt makers to create original patterns and offers an example of extensive drafting with rewarding results. This copy was executed by the donor in 1933.

84 in. square   A-665

Gift of Mrs. Charlotte Jane Whitehill

48

Rose Tree, 1940, is bold in design and color. An elaborate border often referred to as *Melon* or *Hammock* encloses the nine semicircular rose sprays. Colors of pink and rose are dominant with touches of yellow and green applied for leaves and stems. A simple square design is employed in the quilting stitches.

90 in. square

A-654

Gift of Mrs. Charlotte Jane Whitehill

The Technique of Quilting

Having made the top of the quilt, regardless of type, the toil of quilting is yet another challenge. From the time the first books on needlework were written, little was recounted of the stitchery involved in the process of quilting. Consequently, the women engaged in this arduous undertaking were forced to invent the needlework patterns which united the tripart quilt. The imaginative creativity of these needleworkers resulted in an immense diversity of stitchery, ranging from the simple diamond or square to the elaborate plumes and vines.

Parallel rows of tiny running stitches formed the geometric designs in the early works. Later such embellishments as pineapples, harps, vines, shells, hearts and flowers were introduced as quilting patterns. Ideally, quilting stitches were one-sixteenth of an inch in length!

The composition is "laid on" prior to attaching the quilt to the frame, or it can be marked as the quilting progresses. It is believed the latter was customary in early quilts as space did not permit the former. Today, templates and other mechanical devices produce perfect patterns, far surpassing the patterns developed by Colonial women who employed common household tools. Pencils are used to trace the patterns on light colors, while chalk or soap define the design on dark tones.

Quilting Bees of the 19th century were major social events. With the advent of spring, after having spent long winter months completing the tops, the ladies sent out invitations for "Quilt Her Tops" parties. The culinary aptitude of the hostess was essential as supper time was the signal for a festive board, filled with taste-tempting dishes. Husbands, brothers and sweethearts gathered for a convivial evening following the task-filled day of quilting.

49

Ohio Rose, 1922, was copied from one of the oldest patterns which dates from Colonial times. The major difference between this example and that on the facing page is easily recognized in the quilting application which is a highly decorative series of circles and semicircles, a distinct complement to the crisp authority of the red and white gingham and the solid red, green and black cottons. The border, while similar to that of number 48, has a delicate quality. Its name, *Lover's Knot* or *Looped Ribbons* is well chosen.

84 in. square

A-653

Gift of Mrs. Charlotte Jane Whitehill

50 and 51

Rose Bud is a blending of two shades of pink with a bright spring green used for the buds which surround each of the 20 blossoms. This pattern is one of the many rose designs and is sometimes called *Democratic Rose,* an updating of the original *Whig Rose.* This is another example of a combination of piecing to achieve the flowers and appliqué for the attachment to the ground. The introduction of embroidery is unique and gives a lifelike quality to the tiny buds, almost as if they were growing. The donor credits Miss Sadie Crabtree of El Dorado, Kansas, with the quilt making and Mrs. Emma Clawson of Wichita, Kansas, with the quilting. As noted previously (illus. 40, 41) Mrs. Danner at one time published quilting information, and in the book in which this quilt is illustrated one of her helpful hints to quilt makers pertained to scallops which she prefers to do when the quilting is complete. To accomplish this for one quilt, she cuts one-half yard of material on the bias one inch wide. Another of her helpful suggestions is never to leave selvage on the materials as it is not possible to take small stitches through a selvage.

94 x 77 in.   A-1914
Gift of Mrs. Scioto Imhoff Danner, Newton, Kansas

52 and 53

There are many distinctive features worth noting in this quilt. It was made by the donor's great-grandmother, Margaret Neff, who quilted her name and the date, 1856, near the center. Also quilted is the outline of a baby's hand. Although it takes a sharp eye to locate any of these identifying marks, they are indeed there!

84 in. square

A-2109
Gift of Mrs. T. H. Ingley

54 and 55

This is a very intricate appliqué made up of 16 blocks with a 12-inch border. The blocks are similar to *Oak Leaf, Hickory Leaf* and *Reel* patterns. The particularly fine quilting is done in various patterns: shell, diamond, squares, and diagonals. Green feathered plumes interspersed with red roses grace the border.

90 x 98 in.   A-2058

Gift of Mrs. Ruth Newlon

56, 57 and 58

Yellow Rose Wreath was executed by the donor in 1943. The center wreath measures about a yard in circumference with twining green leaves and monochromatic yellow blossoms and buds interspersed. The overlaid appliqué gives the roses a three dimensional quality as illustrated in the detail above. Also evident are the very fine stitches in both the appliqué and the quilting. The four corners are quilted with an elaborate leaf spray done in feather quilting.

89 x 91 in.

A-659

Gift of Mrs. Charlotte Jane Whitehill

59 and 60

Indiana Wreath was made in 1930, the second year of the donor's quilt making career. Unlike her other wreath designs, this one is a veritable flower garden of color! Three shades of green, three purples used for the grapes, five different calicoes and seven additional plain colors result in a vibrant composition. *Princess Feather* quilting outlines the central wreath and expands into a plume in each corner. To achieve this complex quilting, 1,210 yards of thread were used.

90 in. square

A-660

Gift of Mrs. Charlotte Jane Whitehill

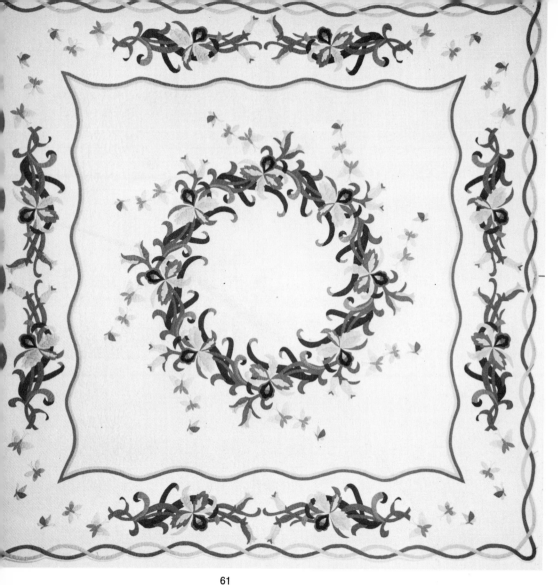

61

Orchid Wreath was a popular pattern early in the century. The original design was made in 1929 by Mrs. Rose G. Kretsinger and copied by Mrs. Whitehill in 1933. As in previous patterns, the *Princess Feather* quilting adorns the corners and encircles the wreath.

82 in. square

A-658

Gift of Mrs. Charlotte Jane Whitehill

62
Poppies, 1895, is different from the familiar interpretation which
uses a row of poppies for the border. Three delicate shades of
pink are used with a single green for leaves and stems.
72 x 84 in. A-628
Gift of Mrs. George Vallery

63 and 64

The *Bride's Quilt* was a tradition of the 19th century when it was also referred to as an *Album Quilt.* Friends worked a favorite pattern and then assembled their combined efforts, thus giving the bride a collection of diverse patterns to pursue. This example executed in 1945 was taken from a quilt given to a bride in the Lennartson family, c. 1850. With permission to copy the heirloom, Mrs. Whitehill quite naturally exhibited a consistency of needlework which was not possible in the original with the multiple quilters.

83. in. square

A-666

Gift of Mrs. Charlotte Jane Whitehill

65 and 66

Cherry Tree dates from 100 years before this version was created in 1936. Each branch of the four trees has approximately 50 different pieces, which gives some indication of the intricacy involved in making this delightful quilt. Each of the cherries was padded before being applied. It was common practice with such complicated patterns to keep the quilting stitches simple, in this case irregularly spaced diagonal lines.

82 in. square   A-682

Gift of Mrs. Charlotte Jane Whitehill

67 and 68

This version of *Winged Square* is a quilt top which was appliquéd in Pekin, Illinois, in 1897 by Mrs. Mary Haas, who in turn gave it to Mary Katherine Schalk on the occasion of her marriage to Joseph L. Hart in that same year. Red and white calico so typical of that period is combined with a natural cotton muslin. The top was quilted in 1972 by a church group in San Francisco.

72 x 87 in.

A-2028

Gift of Irene H. Brown, San Francisco

69 and 70

Snow Flake is composed of 12 blue flakes on a white ground, bordered on all four sides by the reverse pattern of white on blue. Made in 1940, the colors are so well selected that the impression of snow crystals is immediate. Padding is heavier than usual, so undoubtedly the quilt was intended for winter use. To unify the overall piece, quatrefoil quilting patterns are systematically repeated.

82 x 93 in.   A-667

Gift of Mrs. Charlotte Jane Whitehill

71 and 72

Autumn Leaf is a design which won first prize at the Chicago World's Fair in 1893. Mrs. Whitehill copied it in 1934, substituting yellow for the pink used in the original. In the center, where there are approximately 115 leaves, there is no duplication of calicoes The four inch strip around the center section has repeat, padded leaf forms. The sawtooth edge was made by overlapping triangles of different colored materials.

88 x 99 in.   A-657

Gift of Mrs. Charlotte Jane Whitehill

73 and 74

Flowers and birds, very whimsical in character and with a strong chinoiserie influence, are executed in shades of brown, blue and rose. The ground is a fine unbleached muslin. The backing is of a coarser variety and no batting has been used. The curved lower corners and the size indicate that this was made for a bedspread. English, 19th century.

104 x 93 in.   E-1398

On loan from Mrs. Amy S. Goodell, Berkeley, California

75

This elaborately quilted piece incorporates an intricate center medallion with a *Feather* or *Princess Plume* design gracefully curving inside the colored border. Pinks and purples are used in the roses and grapes, with a dark red for birds.

92 in. square

A-674

Gift of Mrs. Charlotte Jane Whitehill

Introduction to Coverlets

The origin of weaving has been traced to prehistoric days through Egyptian hieroglyphics and grave pieces from China. Which of these cultures can rightfully be credited with the actual introduction of the art is still open to question.

Puritan women introduced weaving to America from England in the 17th century. Out of this folk art tradition have come the excellent examples of 18th and 19th century coverlets which exist today.

Women worked in the fields hoeing, planting and gathering the cotton which they then carded and spun. It was the women too who sheared, washed and carded the wool in preparation for home-dyeing. Roots were dug, bark collected from trees, and flowers dried with loving care to produce colors to be used. New England coverlets were conservative with the imported indigo and madder dyes supplying the basic colors. In the South weavers were more adventuresome and introduced shades of rose, green and yellow. The synthetic dyes that became available about 1869 gave a far wider range of color but lacked the softness of the vegetable dyes.

The loom dominated the common room in the early homes. As the house was enlarged, the loom was moved from this area to a less conspicuous location. In the South and Midwest, weaving houses were constructed behind the main residence in the service grounds. The loom house at Mount Vernon still stands.

The coverlet was a necessary part of everyday life for the beauty it brought into the household and its contribution to warmth. As with quilts, the names of patterns were inspired by nature, city or state of origin, seasons, and political and historical happenings. There are probably more names than patterns because several names were often applied to the same pattern.

Professional weavers came from Europe to the Colonies where they held a very prestigious position in the community. These weavers signed their names in either of the lower corners along with the date, location and, very rarely, the name of the person for whom the coverlet was woven. Certain motifs used by these men identified their country of origin. Thistle and heather identified the Scot whereas the lion or eagle was closely associated with English weavers. Other nationalities migrating to America were German, French and Irish.

Coverlets in the collection of the Denver Art Museum number close to 50 and the collection continues to grow through the generosity of donors.

Overshot Coverlets

Colonial weavers in the United States seem to have limited their artistic endeavors to the four-harness loom, a fact which accounts for the multiformity of repetitive geometric patterns found in the overshot coverlets. Records indicate that most of these originated in New York State.

Drafts were a combination of stripes, diamonds and squares with the warp of a natural linen and the weft a single-color homespun wool. The result was as psychedelic as any contemporary painting or strobe light extravaganza. In this technique "skips" or "floats" of weft are woven over a tabby foundation. This is often referred to as a supplementary weft.

Two woven strips of two yards or more in width vary in lengths that average 90 inches. Precise seaming is the hallmark of an able artisan as is apparent in the following examples.

Names describe the design, sometimes with a stretch of the imagination, and most often they are fanciful. As with quilts, the same pattern is known by various titles depending on the point of origin. *Double Bow Knot,* for example, has as many as 15 name variations.

The Denver Art Museum collection in this category is comprehensive in both design and color. However, the imported indigo and madder dyes predominate throughout.

76 and 77
This coverlet carries a variation of the *Sunrise* pattern. Woven in two shades of brown plus gold, the weaving creates an optical effect of flickering light not unlike that of the rising sun. Two-ply cotton and wool yarns were used on a four-harness loom. Made about 1775, its origin is probably New York State.
73 x 96 in., seamed   A-805
                                                  Museum Purchase

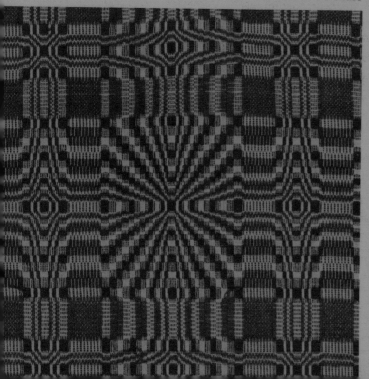

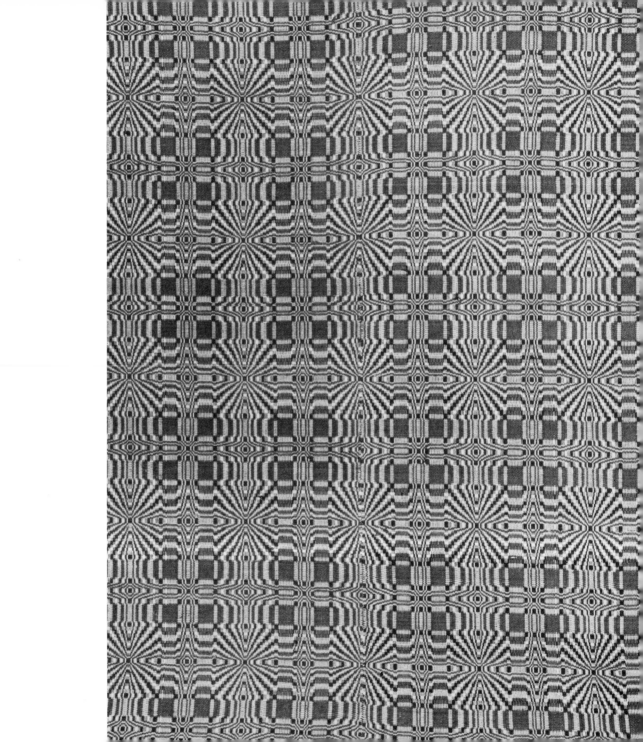

78 and 79

This coverlet is recorded by the donor to have been made in North Carolina by relatives of her grandfather, who left the state about 1852. The indigo and white design, a common pattern, has a variety of names but is most often referred to as *Double Chariot Wheels* or *Church Windows*. The coverlet has a fine single-ply tabby weft with a single-ply linen warp.

65 x 75 in.   A-1434a

Gift of Mrs. Elizabeth Craven

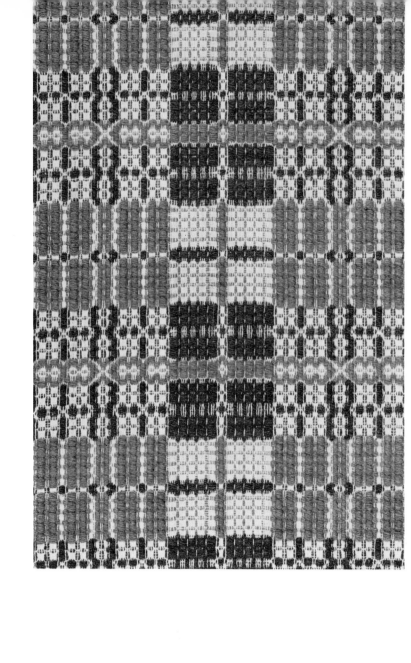

80 and 81

This coverlet dating from early to mid-19th century carries a design which is similar to the *Patch Pattern* compositions. A four-harness loom was used for the weaving with a fine single-ply tabby wool for the weft and a cotton warp. An example of the overshot type, the coverlet has a warp fringe. The vegetable dyes in shades of green could have come from butternuts, and most likely the tan came from cotton flowers. The pattern is repeated 12 times horizontally.

102 x 90 in.

A-1057

Gift of Mr. and Mrs. Robert Bates

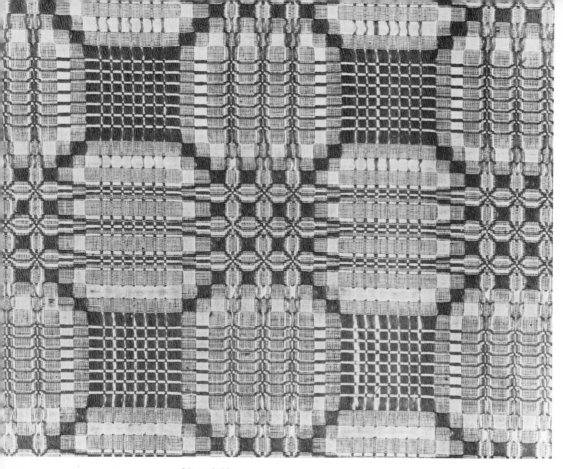

82 and 83

As is so frequently the case, the pattern of this coverlet has been known by many different names including: *Pine Bloom, Star of the Sea* and *Isle of Patmos*. Another four-harness coverlet, this has a single-ply linen warp and a tabby weft. The geometric checkered forms are bent into soft curves by optical illusion. Madder (*Rubia tinctorum*) was a particularly popular dye, second only to indigo. Made in two strips, the coverlet is seamed down the center.

69 x 87 in.

A-898
Gift of Miss Elizabeth Blanc

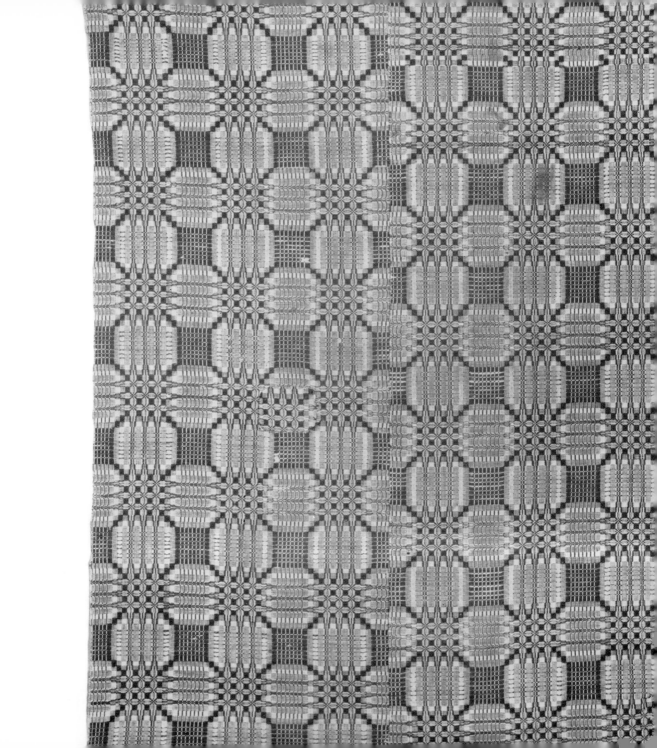

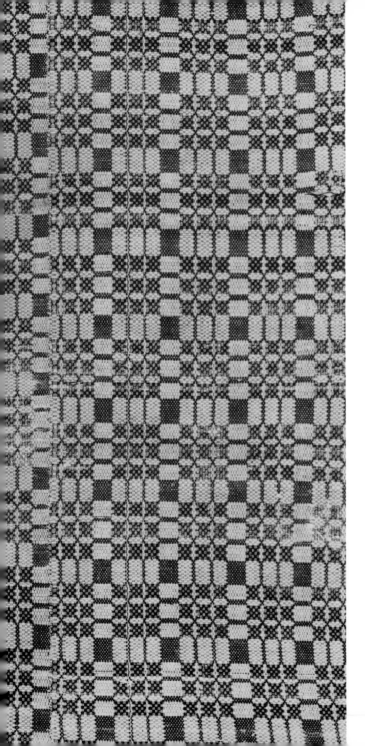

84 and 85
Table or patch areas surround the standard nine-star pattern in this wool and cotton overshot coverlet. The typical combination of indigo and white is reversible. Loom setup for this pattern would have been four-block, four-harness with the white carrying the warp and the weft the blue.
61 x 74 in., seamed   A-725
Gift of Mrs. Frederic H. Douglas

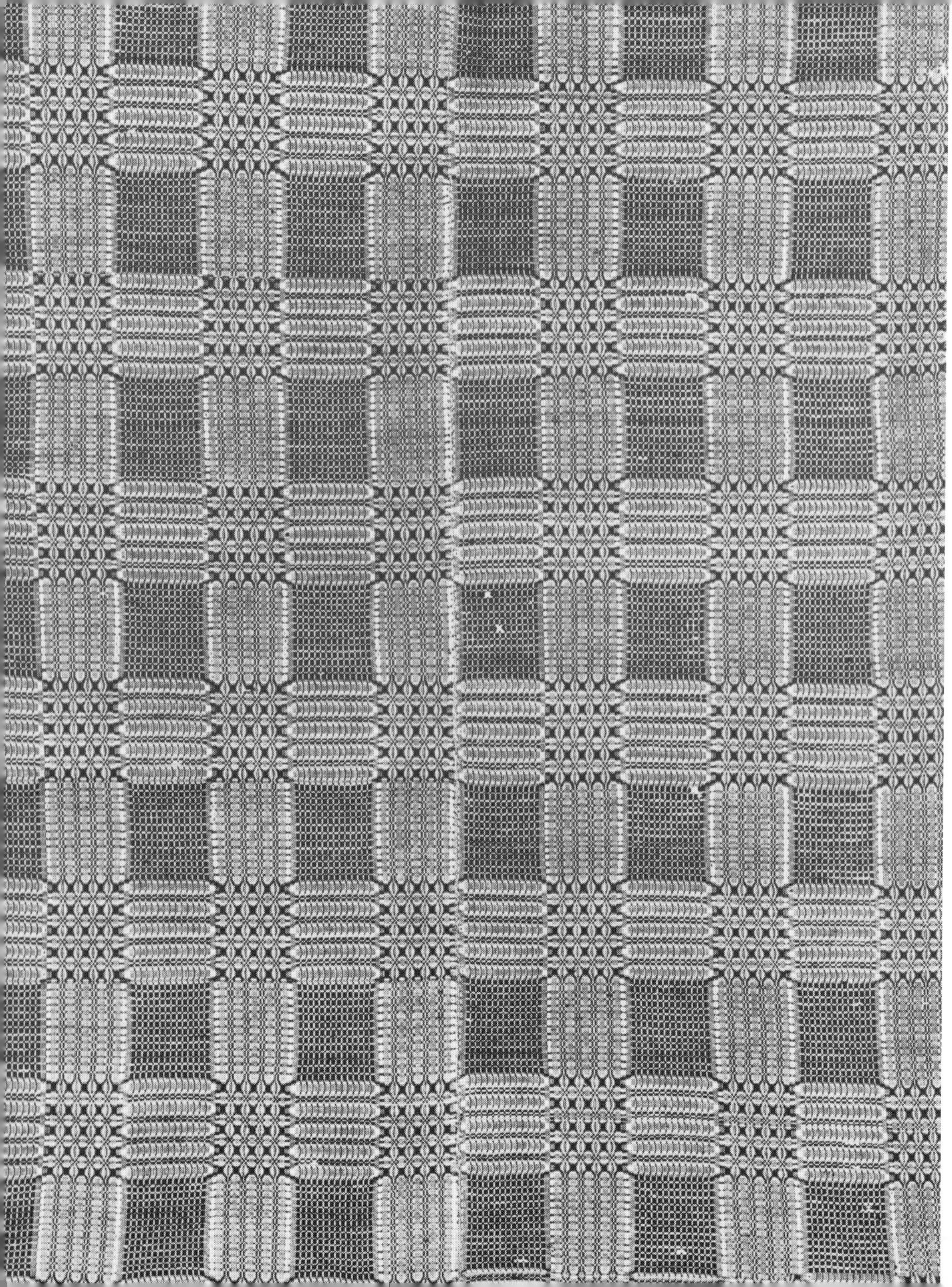

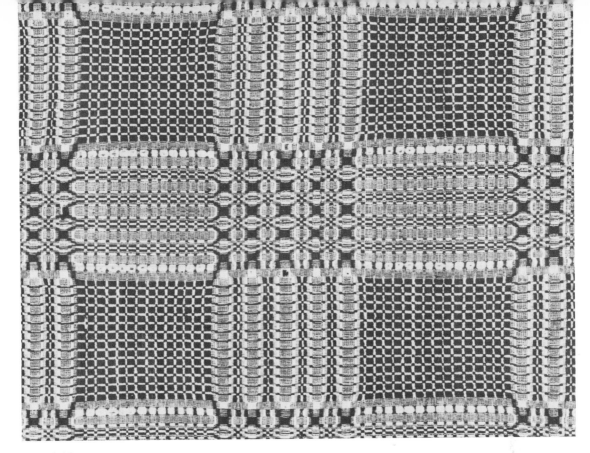

86 and 87

Home-woven coverlets have a certain charm in color and design and are usually easy to identify. In this instance, the typical blue blends well with another wool in a rose shade and off-white cotton warps. *Stars* and *Tables* alternate in the pattern. Single-ply yarns, as used in this overshot example, indicate that the work was done in the early 1800's.

88 x 72 in., seamed

A-174

Gift of Mrs. Charles Bonfils

88 and 89

In a collection of some 75 coverlets it is amazing that there is only one example of *Summer-and-Winter*. Believed to be of American origin, the technique has been the center of dispute. Some consider this type to be a coverlet which is actually double-woven with a dark and light side. Others believe it to be a three-over-one-under method in which the pattern advances with each throw of the shuttle, a technique which creates no solid areas. This mosiac pattern was executed on a six-harness loom with a two-ply cotton warp and a two-ply wool weft.

75 x 184 in., seamed

A-1407
Gift of Miss Ina T. Aulls

90 and 91
This handwoven coverlet is a typical example of a double-weave. The pyramiding squares in the center are indigo on one side and white on the other. The pattern, often referred to as *Doors and Windows,* was achieved with a four-block, 16-harness loom. All wool, the coverlet is dated in the early 1800's.
77 x 65 in., seamed

A-165
Gift of Mrs. S. Effie Parkhill

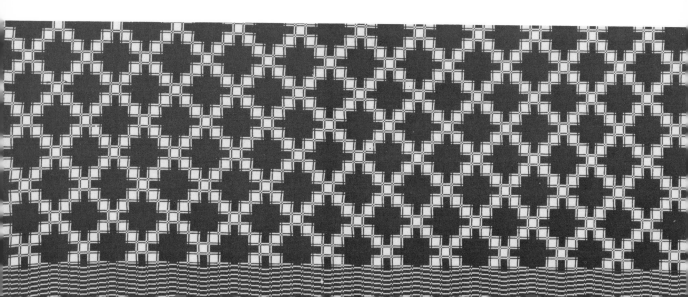

Double-Weave Coverlets

During the middle period of American weaving, double-weave, often referred to as double-face or double-cloth, reached its zenith. Looms became more elaborate than the earlier cottage loom as the complexity of the technique required a more sophisticated mechanism. The eight-harness loom produced the simplest patterns; thus twelve or more harnesses (in multiples of four) make possible the more complicated drafts.

Most patterns in this category were derived from the natural environment which accounts for the variety of tree forms, stars and snowballs. Other patterns such as the *Lover's Knot* and the *Wheel of Fortune* are rooted in Victorian sentiment.

Pennsylvania was the origin of most of these simple geometric designs credited to the Mennonite weavers. However, the earliest documented double-weave, dated 1805, was executed by James Alexander, a professional weaver in New York, who is credited with innumerable coverlets and carpets in this weave. His production continued until 1824.

Colors are almost universally the same in the double-weave coverlets, with natural cotton predominating in both warp and weft, accompanied with an indigo or madder weft. Thread count is fairly consistent, varying an average of six to ten in both directions of construction.

92 and 93
Eight-point star medallions are intertwined with vine patterns in this coverlet, a fairly common design. The acorn double border is also a familiar pattern in this period. Dating 1840-50, this is made with a linen and wool base in natural color and blue.
81 x 76 in., seamed

A-483
Gift of Mrs. Susan Conklin

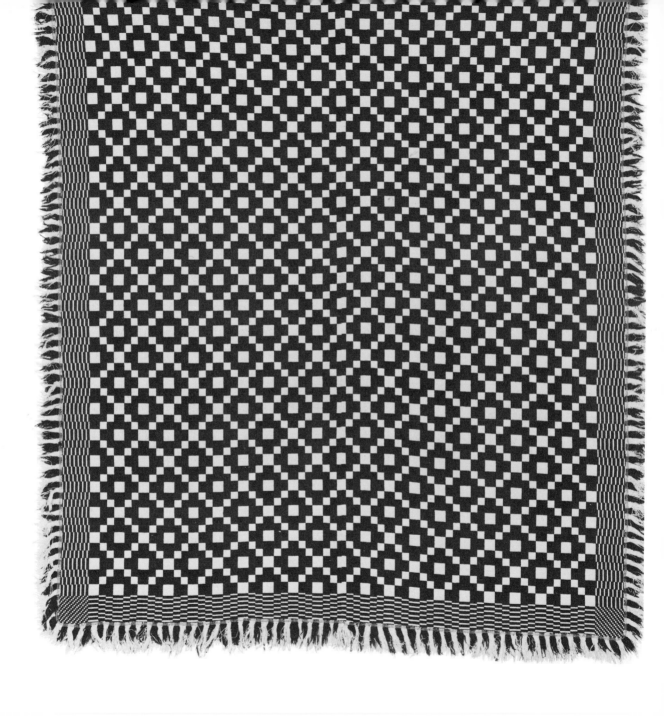

94, opposing page
This indigo and white double handwoven coverlet of linen and wool has a four-inch fringe on three sides. Of Pennsylvania origin and dating c. 1775, this coverlet probably was made on a three-block, 12-harness loom setup.
78 x 90 in., seamed   A-729
                              Gift of Mrs. Frederic H. Douglas

95, at right
Rose blossoms surrounded by leaves is a common design but the construction is questionable. As there is no seam, the blue and white wool coverlet was probably executed on a two-person loom. It is of Pennsylvania origin.
87 x 74 in.   A-820
                              Gift of Mrs. Marion Byles Grove

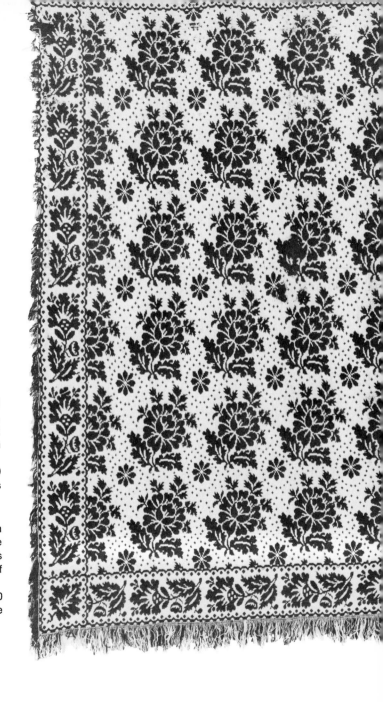

96 and 97

This geometric pattern is early 18th century. The units, running ten across and 13 down, are stylized snowflakes executed in white, indigo and rose. Such rose shades usually came from types of lichen or a grapevine-based dye. The twill block in the border design and the overall pattern was done on a five-block, 20-harness setup. Obviously most of the fringe is lost.

70 x 82 in., seamed   A-624

Gift of Mrs. George Kenmore

98, opposing page

Pine tree borders were very common in 19th century coverlets. Often the trees were slender as if reaching towards the heavens. In the center section of the coverlet the repeat patterns are feathery snowflakes. Indigo, rose and white is the color combination in this five-block, 20-harness coverlet.

66 x 77 in., seamed   A-157

Gift of Mrs. O. E. Caray

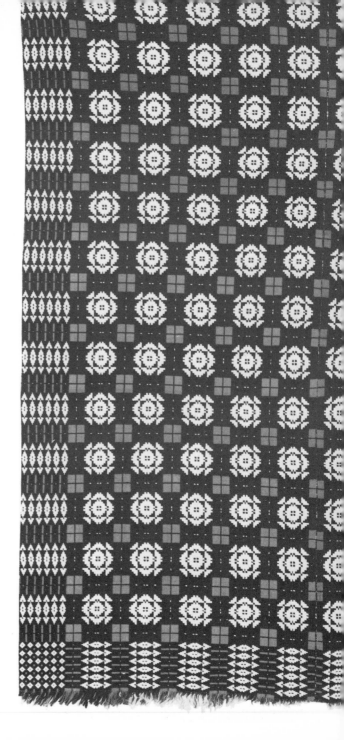

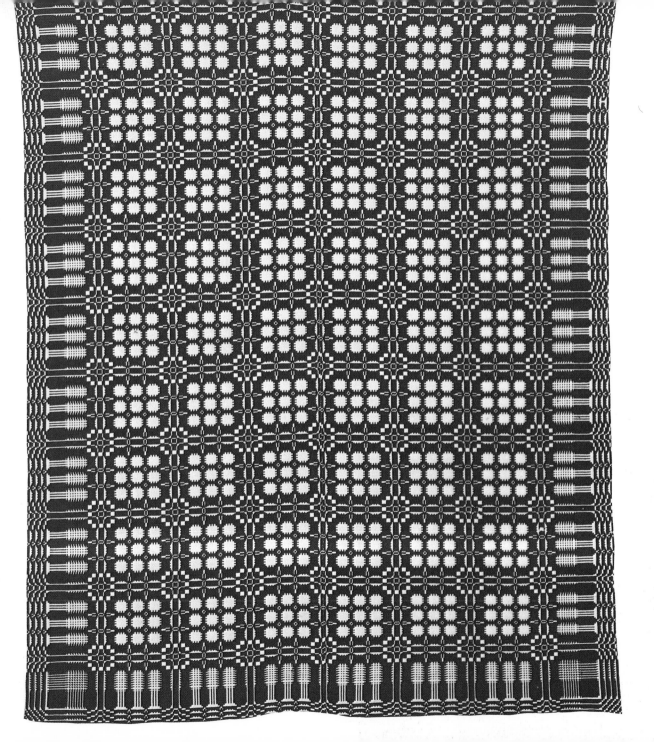

99 and 100

This overall pattern of indigo, rose and white incorporates squares, circles, and diamonds in a pleasantly symmetrical, geometric pattern. The pine tree border which is used frequently was inspired by the Pine Tree shilling minted in the 17th century. Both warp and weft are homespun wool, vegetable dyed.

66 x 77 in., seamed   A-157

Gift of Mrs. O. E. Caray

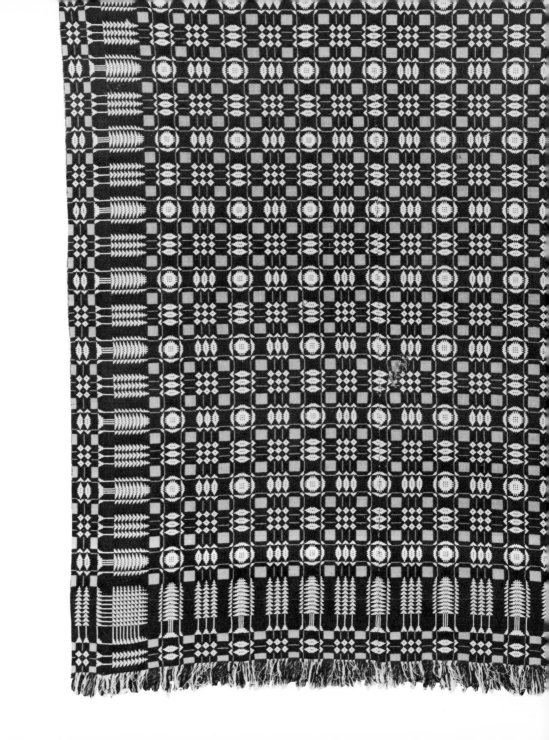

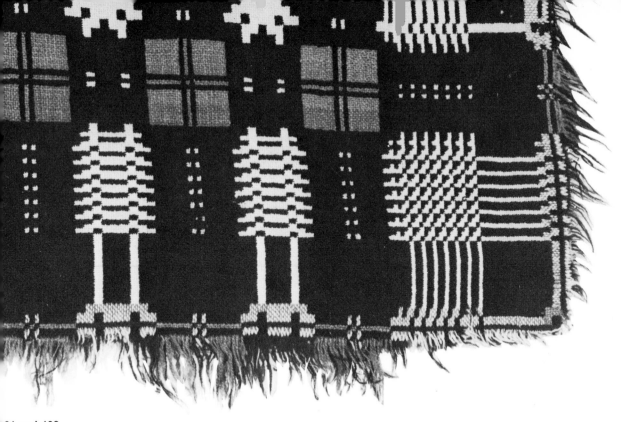

01 and 102

This is another version of snowflakes in the same indigo, rose and white
s previous examples of double-woven coverlets. Here the pine tree
order is not so exaggerated. The precision of the craftsmanship suggests
hat an itinerant or professional weaver executed this piece. The pattern
alls for a four-block, 16-harness loom setup.

6 x 80 in., seamed

A-168

Gift of Mrs. S. Effie Parkhill

103 and 104

Coverlets with cotton and wool content did not hold their shape as well as wool or linen and wool, as evidenced here in a very common blue and white example. The coverlet has a warp fringe bottom, selvage sides and a hemmed top. Units of white squares like those in this pattern are often referred to as *Windows*. Five-block, 20-harness.

70 x 76 in., seamed   A-1071b

Gift of Lilian Montrose Grahame Estate, Fort Collins, Colorado

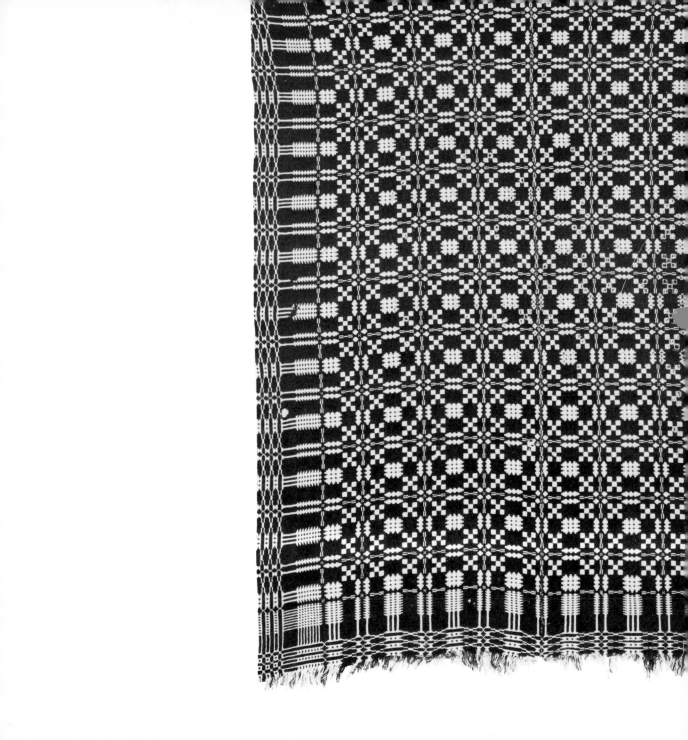

105 and 106

Another variation of the pine tree design is found in this double-weave coverlet with a color combination of white and madder. The latter color came from a dye more common to Europe than America because the colonists did not have time to cultivate dyestuffs. This yellow powder results from grinding the root of the plant *Rubia tinctorum* and then allowing the substance to ferment in order to achieve greater pigmentation. The coverlet has knotted warp fringe on the bottom and is sewn on the sides. That this is credited to Pennsylvania is reasonable as it was the German settlers who introduced the double-weave into the United States.

84 x 95 in., seamed   A-721

Gift of Mrs. Frederic H. Douglas

107 and 108

The weaver's interpretation of the *Nine Snowball* design is a most unusual one in this double-weave coverlet. The pattern is so small that it is difficult to separate the layers. The borders are also much wider than usual and the introduction of raspberry color with the blue and white is yet another variation. Currants and huckleberries were the usual sources for such a reddish dye. It is a four-block, 16-harness weave, hemmed on both sides and with a bound selvage.

66 x 96 in., seamed

A-723

Gift of Mrs. Frederic H. Douglas

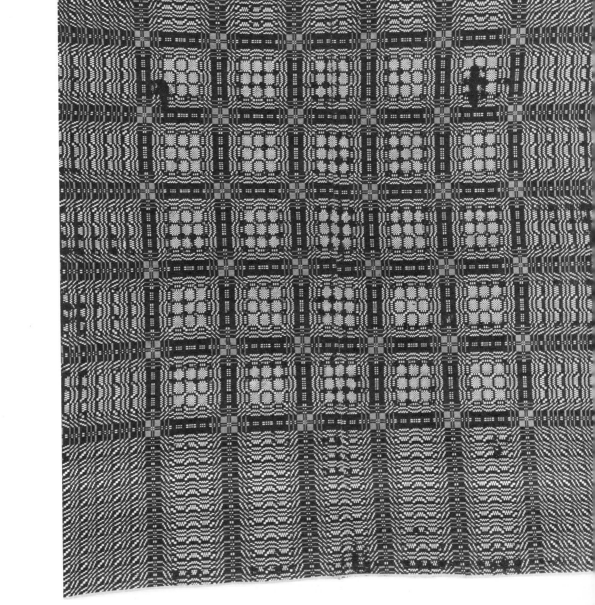

109 and 110
Lilies and stars are repeated in many ways in the Jacquard coverlets, which lend themselves to elaborate patterns. In this example two-ply wools are used in blue, red, and natural yarns.
76 x 83 in., seamed

A-225
Museum Purchase

Jacquard Coverlets

Over a period of some 75 years, several French inventors were at work on developing a sophisticated loom, capable of producing extremely complex patterns. It was Joseph Jacquard who finalized the loom which carries his name. The unlimited patterns possible on this machine brought about a drastic advancement in the making of coverlets.

The loom was first demonstrated at the Paris Industrial Exhibition in 1801 and arrived in America 19 years later. Punched cards, not unlike today's computer methods, activated the loom to create elaborate patterns. Needles traveling through the holes on the cards separately controlled an average of 40 pounds of homespun, with as many as 2,000 warp threads.

The earliest Jacquard coverlets still had the center seam but the later looms were larger and allowed for the one-piece coverlets. Identifying these is relatively simple as not only is the overall pattern very elaborate, but borders are especially ornate. A definite French influence is found in most of the design elements, indicating that punched cards did arrive from France with the machines and, as will be noted later, names of patterns also originated there.

Another advantage of this loom was the use of a greater number of colors. Most of the yarns were dyed by women in preparation for the weaver's arrival. The professional weavers who were responsible for most of the Jacquard coverlets traveled from one district to another, weaving to order. Coverlet production averaged three a week although an experienced artisan could produce one a day. For these the cost was ten to twelve dollars.

111 and 112

The master artisan, Peter Uhl, drafted a dramatic combination of lilies, stars, birds and rose trees in this coverlet of 1841. This Jacquard single coverlet carries two white and one blue two-ply wool yarns on the warp with a tabby weft.

72 x 163 in., seamed

A-161

Gift of Mrs. Edna D. Greenamyre

PETER
UHL
TRUMBUL
COUNTY
OHIO.1841

113 and 114

Four roses around a medallion is a common although unnamed pattern in the Jacquards. The red-brown color that is combined with green, dark blue and natural no doubt came from lichen as this was a versatile source for this color family. Lichen were easy to acquire if one walked through the woods on a drizzly day, and they kept very well after harvesting.

78 x 92 in., seamed   A-169

Gift of Mrs. S. Effie Parkhill

115 and 116

Floral medallions dominate the center portion of this indigo and white reversible single Jacquard coverlet with grapevines twining throughout the three-sided border. The binding at the top is handwoven in shades of red and yellow and it appears to be original. The indigo plant which produces the yellow juices which in turn produce the deep blue so common in coverlets was first developed in the Orient during Marco Polo's time. This is an excellent dye for both cotton and wool.

92 x 70 in., seamed   A-164

Gift of Mrs. S. Effie Parkhill

J. PACKER &
C. DOUGLASS
BROWNSVI-
-LLE. 1838.

117 and 118

The conspicuous star form centered in this quilt is a yard wide and very boldly executed in blue on white. Delicate vines in the field surrounding the star only add to its boldness. Cartouche designs with plumes, scrolls and sprays of flowers decorate the corners. The ornate patterns reveal a French influence. The wear of the piece indicates that the quilt was a household favorite.

87 x 83 in.

A-581
Gift of Robert Wegg

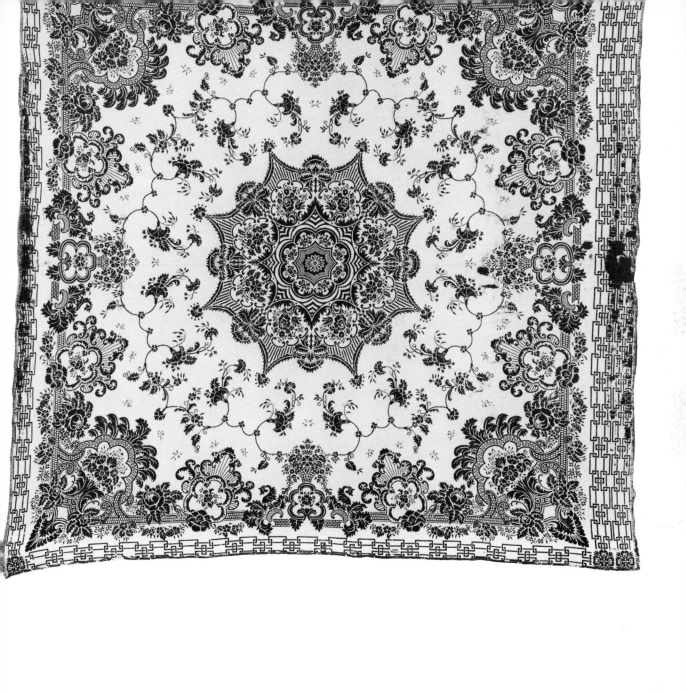

COVERLET.
WM.H.VAN-
GORDON.
WEAVER.
COVINGTON
MIAMI. CO.
OHIO.1852.

119 and 120
Color is as important as design in this flower-strewn reversible coverlet.
The colors have been shot across the warp in a very even manner with
no regard for the pattern they cross. The professional weaver has
meticulously placed the corner information. More often than not this was
done with little regard for spacing. Made of linen and wool.
72 x 92 in., seamed   A-331
                                               Gift of Mrs. Ray Summer

COVERLET.
WM H. VAN
GORDON.
COVINGTON
MIAMI CO.
OHIO 1852

121 and 122

From the corner information, one finds that this coverlet was created in Wooster, Ohio, in 1845 by Peter Hartman. During this period of our country's history, Wooster was a large Amish community. A coverlet in the collection of the Art Institute of Chicago is credited to J. Hartman, dated 1840, and executed in Milton Township, Ohio. It was common for families engaged in weaving to travel together, so it can be assumed that these two Hartmans were related. Roosters, an emblem of the Democratic Party in 1844, appear in the side borders.

77 x 89 in.   A-724

Gift of Mrs. Frederic H. Douglas

123 and 124
Lilies and stars form the ground design of this coverlet dated 1846.
Various kinds of birds are interspersed with weeping willow trees in the
three border sections. Home-dyed wool and cotton are reversible in
tan and blue.
72 x 90 in., seamed

A-284
Gift of Mrs. Arthur Cassidy

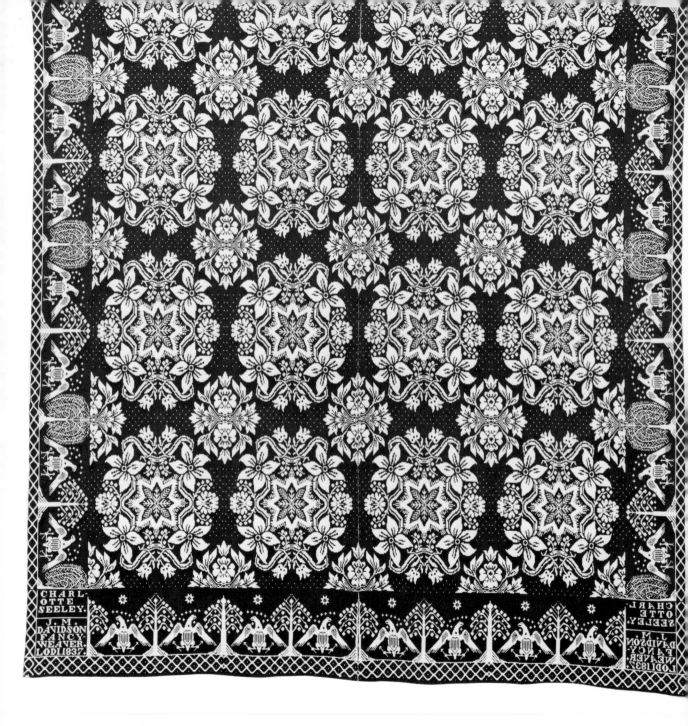

CHARL-
OTTE
SEELEY.

J.M.
DAVIDSON
FANCY
WEAVER
LODI 1837

125 and 126

Yet another artisan's interpretation of *Lilies and Stars* uses the lily medallion referred to as *Lilies of France*. The liberty border is well laid out in eagle and tree designs. This double Jacquard consists of two-ply natural and blue wool in both warp and weft. According to the donor, the coverlet was made in Lodi, New York.

78 x 84 in., seamed

A-818
Gift of Mary Willsea

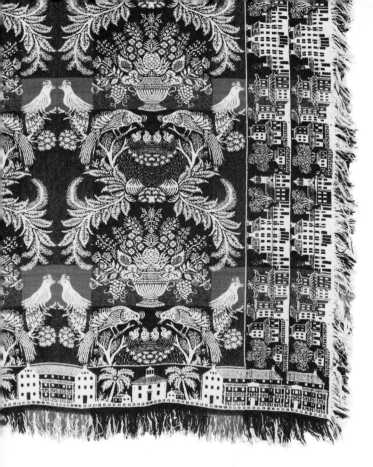

127 and 128

This design was very popular during the mid-1800's and was usually woven in blue and red wool with natural linen. It is known as *Birds of Paradise* and also as *Penelope's Flower Pot.* The border carries the *Boston Town* pattern. There are two in the Denver Art Museum collection with the only variance being in the shape of the flower urns. Both are Jacquard double-weave and both have the same measurements.

91 x 86 in.   A-733

Gift of Mrs. Frederic H. Douglas

129 and 130

Unfortunately only one-half of this Jacquard single-weave remains. It is very lightly woven with as many as ten carry-overs in the weft. Lilies and stars are the subject of the design with a grapevine border separated from the main field with arrows. Colors are black and blue wool and white cotton. Yellow iris were the most readily available source for black dye.

39 x 95 in.

A-228

Gift of Dr. and Mrs. Byron E. Cohn

131 and 132
Flower medallions are enclosed in octagonal units on this indigo and white coverlet in a pattern which closely resembles *Frenchman's Fancy*. The borders are copied from *Thistles and Lilies* with the lilies twining on side borders and thistles along the fringed bottom.

74 x 100 in., seamed A-1927
Gift of Mrs. Mary Wade Beckley
in memory of her mother
Elizabeth McIntosh Wade

133 and 134

Although the *Bird of Paradise* pattern originated in New York, the donors have documentation that this example was made in Pennsylvania and belonged to a family by the name of Herbzt. The pattern shows a strong Dutch-Germanic influence. Warp is natural cotton and weft is a combination of the same cotton and red and yellow ocher wool.

87 x 78 in.   A-1682

      Gift of Mr. and Mrs. Fred Collins

135 and 136

Evenly spaced feathers and medallions create the impression of many squares with the motifs superimposed on them. Dark blue and bright rose are interwoven to create a purple tweed in combination with a two-ply white linen in the warp. The effect is much like that of printed patterns from India. Fringed garland borders decorate three sides.

70 x 76 in., seamed   A-1071a

Gift from the Lilian Montrose Grahame
Estate, Fort Collins, Colo.

137 and 138

Flower medallions and stylized roses repeat in the highly concentrated design in this Jacquard coverlet. Conventional indigo wool and natural linen have been used in this 1846 example. Thistle borders appear on either side with symmetric bird and tree patterns across the bottom. The seaming is very accurate although some areas are badly worn.

80 x 85 in., seamed

A-2141

Gift of Mrs. Frazer Arnold

139 and 140

Trees, roses and stars appear in shades of blue, rose and yellow ocher. Although variations of the designs found in this coverlet have been repeated numerous times, the composition here leads one to believe that this is an original design by the weaver. The signed corners are most irregular, for they do not read correctly on either side at what should be the bottom of the quilt. The detail illustrated here has been placed upside down for this reason.

84 x 72 in., seamed

A-2013
Gift of Ruth Robinson

141 and 142
This green coverlet was woven by J. Gamble, a professional Irish weaver. There are othe[r]
by the name of Gamble recorded as weavers in Kentucky during the 1830's. There are se[v]
eral ways to achieve the color of green used in this coverlet. A common source is the leave[s]
from the privet shrub, or it can also be attained by dyeing indigo over yellow. The draft o[f]
this coverlet is well organized and planned to incorporate the seam into the design. Th[e]
initials "E. B." are embroidered on the necks of the two doves in the center of the uppe[r]
border. These probably designate the individual for whom the coverlet was woven in 183[4].
78 x 86 in., seamed

A-8[0]
Museum Purchas[e]

J.G.AMBLE
WEAVER.
1834

143 and 144

The colors in this coverlet vary from previously illustrated Jacquards executed in stripes of color. Here indigo, rose and light green wools are worked on a natural linen warp. Twenty flower medallions form the center ground with flower and leaf designs evenly interspersed. The handsewn binding appears to be much later than the coverlet and was probably added when the self-fringe became badly worn.

76 x 88 in., seamed

A-2029

Gift of Jean Williams

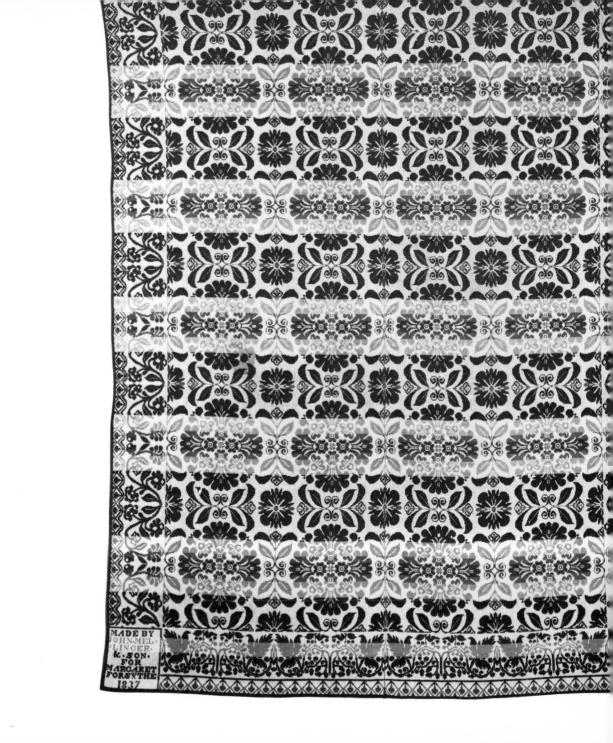

MADE BY
JOHN MEL-
LINGER
& SON.
FOR
MARGARET
FORSYTHE
1837

Bibliography

Carlisle, Lilian Baker. *Pieced Work and Applique Quilts at Shelbourne Museum.* Museum Pamphlet Series, Number 2. Shelbourne, Vermont: 1957.

Colby, Averil. *Quilting.* New York: Charles Scribner's Sons, 1971.

Creekmore, Betsy B. *Traditional American Crafts.* New York: Hearthside Press, Inc., 1968.

Danner, Mrs. Scioto Imhoff. *Mrs. Danner's Quilts.* Third, Fourth and Fifth Books. El Dorado, Kansas: 1954, 1958, 1970.

Davison, Mildred, and Mayer-Thurman, Christa C. *Coverlets.* Chicago, Illinois: Art Institute of Chicago, 1973.

Dunham, Lydia Roberts. *Denver Art Museum Quilt Collection.* Denver, Colorado: 1963.

Eaton, Allen H. *Handicrafts of New England.* New York: Bonanza Books, n. d.

Fennelly, Catherine. *Textiles in New England, 1790-1840.* Sturbridge, Mass.: Old Sturbridge Village, 1961.

Frey, Berta. *Four Harness Weaving.* West Hartford, Conn.: Handweavers Guild of America, Inc., 1972.

Hall, Carrie A., and Kretsinger, Rose G. *The Romance of the Patchwork Quilt in America.* New York: Bonanza Books, 1935.

Hall, Eliza Calvert. *A Book of Handwoven Coverlets.* Tokyo, Japan, and Rutland, Vermont: Charles E. Tuttle Co., 1966.

Holstein, Jonathan. *The Pieced Quilt — An American Design Tradition.* Greenwich, Connecticut: New York Graphic Society, Ltd., 1973.

Gross, Joyce. *A Patch In Time: Catalog of Antique, Traditional and Contemporary Quilts.* Mill Valley, Calif., 1973.

Ickis, Marguerite. *The Standard Book of Quilt Making and Collection.* New York: Dover Publications, 1959.

Jones, Stella M. *Hawaiian Quilts.* Daughters of Hawaii and Honolulu Academy of Arts and Mission Houses Museum, 1973.

Laury, Jean Ray. *Quilts and Coverlets.* New York: Van Nostrand-Reinhold Company, 1970.

McKim, Ruby Short. *One Hundred and One Patchwork Patterns.* New York: Dover Publications, 1962.

Montgomery, Florence M. *Printed Textiles: English and American Cottons and Linens 1700-1850.* New York: The Viking Press, 1970.

Newark Museum. *Hand-woven Coverlets in the Newark Museum.* Newark, New Jersey, 1947.

_____. *Quilts and Counterpanes* in the Newark Museum. Newark, New Jersey, 1948.

Robertson, Sionaid. *Dyes from Plants.* New York: Van Nostrand-Reinhold Company, 1973.

Safford, Carleton, and Bishop, Robert. *America's Quilts and Coverlets.* New York: E. P. Dutton and Company, Inc., 1972.

Victoria and Albert Museum. *Notes on Applied Work and Patchwork.* London, England: Her Majesty's Stationery Office, 1938.

_____. *Notes on Quilting.* London, England: Her Majesty's Stationery Office, 1932.

Photographs by Lloyd Rule, Staff Photographer.

Format suggested by Unit 1, Inc.

This publication has been made possible by a matching grant from the National Endowment for the Arts.